EXISTING SCIENCE

FLETCH FLETCHER

ASSURE PRESS

Copyright © 2021 by Fletch Fletcher

All Rights Reserved. No part of this book may be performed, recorded, used or reproduced in any manner whatsoever without the written consent of the author and the permission of the publisher except in the case of brief quotations embodied in critical articles and review.

An imprint of Assure Press Publishing & Consulting, LLC

www.assurepress.org

ASSURE PRESS

Publisher's Note: Assure Press books may be purchased for educational, business, or sales promotional use. For information please visit the website.

Existing Science/ Fletch Fletcher— 1st ed.

ISBN-13: 978-1-954573-10-9
eISBN-13: 978-1-954573-11-6
Library of Congress Control Number: 2021930008

ACKNOWLEDGMENTS

I am very grateful to the editors of the following journals who did me the honor of publishing poems from this collection:

Euphony Journal
   "Dark Matter Galaxies"

Crack the Spine Literary Magazine
   "Nuclear Deity"

High Shelf Poetry
   "In Orbit"

CONTENTS

1st Law of Motion	1
Fossil Record	2
Nuclear Deity	3
2nd Law of Motion	4
Anywhere you want	5
The Act of Observing	7
Fathers and Biology	8
In Orbit	9
September 14, 2015	10
Dark Matter Galaxies	11
QED	12
1st Law of Thermodynamics	13
Space (& Cells)	14
Least Time	15
Stuff of Life	16
2nd Law of Thermodynamics	17
Cats in Boxes	18
Supernova 2022	19
James Wright in Chemistry Class	20
Radiating Black Bodies	21
3rd Law of Motion	22
Spirit and Opportunity	23
5th Dimension	24
Ode to Offense	25
3rd Law of Thermodynamics	26
Thank you	27
About the Author	29

EXISTING SCIENCE

1ST LAW OF MOTION

for Yesenia Montilla

your Biggie shirt and merengue
feet laugh in inertia's marbled face

the way you flick your panther shine skirt   your fierce
first skin   stepping in every direction

at once   I can't imagine you at rest
now   wild branches of your hair waiting for a hot wind

lover's breath whispering words with Diaz's voice
Neruda's sensuality

no   you never needed a force to move you
music is convenience

your eyes have a voice that sings Adhan
stare   Beyonce style

wait   it isn't your eyes or your mouth or anything
outside   your force is ancient

temples of the body that were built in the dawn
of the first birth   internal force

baffle my science   you are not a hurricane
hurricanes pray to you

Fossil Record

Dig through this dirt skin, delicately.
Touch the bones of all the dead
who made me, all the blood
squeezed into my ribs to keep
breath from breaking me, my jaw as I speak
softly the names of those I never knew,
sixteen fragile bones of my wrists that twist
around each other as I write this.
Keep a record of the stones
stacked in order, in rows, in fields of honor
and fields with forgotten names.
See the missing pieces,
gaps in making me,
but know I was made,
know they were real,
know I love them for being
whatever they were.

Nuclear Deity

Ask me the affinity of Carbon and I'll explain
how your feet form an infinity of empty spaces.

We are Carbon's obsessive compulsion, its four electron arms
bond in desperation, loneliness of atomic separation.
Nuclear bodies never really touch.   Well,

atom smashers, hadron colliders, places
people press the smallest bodies warn us
caresses of small hearts could rip holes in space.

And let's not forget the sun, all its fusion, pure
power. If your feet were made of sun-skin

everywhere you walk would be Heaven.   Where you stop
worlds would grow in circles.   Where you sleep
men would bend knees to pray.   Men would pray
      only when you sleep.

2nd Law of Motion

Newton sort of said size doesn't matter
all that much, but he mixed up
acceleration and excitation.

Never did get his particles right.
Might have thought math spun suns, but,
son, the things a tongue can do
when you take the time

let it map the whole sky
ask how to turn a world and
God, it can be beautiful
if you get a straight answer.

Anywhere you want

If I could wake up tomorrow anywhere
it wouldn't be under this sky

my clouds would be the Pillars of Creation -
open my eyes in a cradle of stars

play nursemaid for a day
to Heaven's brightest lights

I would learn the smell of dark matter
expected to be sweet - like lilac

I would hold red giants in my palms
carry stray protons on my shoulders like atlas

I would bathe on the burning side of a super-earth
tidally locked so the sun shower never ends

I would leave refreshed because
if I could wake anywhere I would wake everywhere

at once, be everything for a day and
in the evening I would walk familiar ground again

having learned the names every star calls itself
and next time I would take you

whoever you are
because I love you

because once you've leaned in to hear
whispered secrets of pulsars

once you've ridden the dark body
below the Horsehead nebula

once you've kissed starlight goodnight

before it fades forever

what could be left to hold from Earth
but love

The Act of Observing

So often
they feel like waves
these children
who stream from the morning busses
crash into room after room
endlessly
cresting and falling back to the bottom of themselves
before folding into the whole of their class and
as one
rolling back into the night
only to return with the sun and flow again
but then you look to one of them
stop the whole
and observe
just for a moment
the piece that is this one body
this one part so content to exist as a wave
and suddenly it is changed
My gaze slows it
crumples it
into a form and for however long I choose
to see this one child that was once lost in the body of a class
I have changed it's outcome
Whatever it would have been
wherever it would have gone
I can never know
because I chose
to know it
more closely.

Fathers and Biology

Everything in biology is female. We named our cells
Mother and *Daughters*, our DNA – the Sisters Chromatid –,
even taxa humans huddle in are feminine
in the original Latin. Nothing of our skin known
as brother, no sons in our blood. X marks the woman's strand,
25,000 genes worth of women in every person's cells.
Men run with Y in their hearts,
a mere handful and maybe shrinking. I see the draw
in names for life-givers, women and their womb,
Mother Earth, but what does that say for the role of fathers?
Must the mother be the only caregiver?
I let my cells turn, embrace the woman who made me, and now I fear
this is science. Will all of me in my children become their mother?
Is there no room for fathers in bone?
Years of searching in his absence
and I've no place in this body for my own.

In Orbit

think *aphelion* and know
why he bundles in dark wool to sleep
the envy of dead
wandering the clothes-cluttered floor
besieging his bed
hiding treasures of coins and bills and cracked plastic
bottles that promised brightness and
barely brought the dim specter
of the moon's borrowed rays
as it too set somewhere in the floorboards and the trail
he left cooled to nothing and even if he could
be warm again it would entail so much
falling

September 14, 2015

The whole of creation convulsed. The sun rippled
like air at the edge of a scream
too distant to hear but
stirs something in your spine
just below the shoulder blades and
if you payed attention you would know
the voice from your bones. Mountains
thinned and stretched and snapped
back and all the September light bowed
ever so subtly in respect to the cries of the universe
that birthed it. I was flipping
through my keys at the top of the six grey steps
to my three floor walk-up when my body waved
with the skin of the world and I saw
nothing but the light
blue of the birthday card from a Grandmother
who never forgets, who I see about as often as mountains
dance to black hole beats.

Dark Matter Galaxies

Dark dwarf galaxies orbit us, spheres so strange
light can't touch them and we can only tell they are waiting
by the pull they have on our bright arms
from our dark halo. If they move too close to the core
tidal waves scatter them, take the majority of mass and cut
drifting ribbons. This is all on paper,
black ink on solid white
wood and glue, and no more a satellite of star clusters than words
around the scar on my left thumb.
Raised, it has sheen in direct sun. I can touch it and know the knife
stroked skin – how a thumb flowed
without rapids – how it opened like evening
primrose. When the needles damned
my tides I saw puffed the fat and bone
fingers are made of. Tell me
there are galaxies in the black,
substance in the void,
even dark matters bleed.

QED

Thus is it perturbed
in the light of day or by the slow
spin of the crescent light of every broken moon.

Prove it to me,
that the way they spin themselves
in every negative direction, the way
they wait in clusters
needing to be near but
never touching, the way
they are so small in their own heads
can be reached.

Tell me the brighter half
of this wholly unnatural world is taken
in by them, these children
of charged homes,
of not-quite mattering
to their cores.

1ST LAW OF THERMODYNAMICS

It isn't true. The universe is growing
cold. Galaxies pull
black to their throats and slip into death
while I sleep. If energy can never be
destroyed, and nothing I create is new,
where has all life's warmth gone?

Maybe I stole it.
Maybe this universe is mine,
and when I pull my own black I'll leave
heat in my left pocket, beside my pen,
86 cents that can't be spent,
a deep grey tie, and unused tissues.

Space (& Cells)

After Kimiko Hahn

I understand space – the emptiness, especially
the black being greater than any star –

distance truly measured in the dark traversed in a year.

I do not understand cells – their fullness,
the distance measured in atoms.

Think neuron: wires made of fat
molecules, dendrites – barkless and bare.

Every thought can't be sodium rush or calcium
waltz. I lose ten-thousand neurons a day.

They rewire dendrite to terminal. I die
when I sleep to wake less in parts.

I don't know the tilt on the sum. How is this
million-trillionth of me translated to the grave?

How could Skove leave in eleventh grade
with more cells than me today? How am I alive

in the gap between synapses?

Least Time

There is a light, a line
cutting some small swath through the universe,
riding one road of infinite option
direct and by far the quickest any ray could know.

I can't see this traveller yet, but I know it
speeds to me,
was set upon me
long before there was a thought of a thought of me.

Maybe it will simply kiss me or
touch me on the shoulder
the way a passerby in a crowd might as she glances
off me, heads back into the black
I'll never know.

Or maybe it will strike me
in the heart, reflect internally
this totality of me, critically, and leave me
brightened,
but it will not.

With respect to every path
I could have taken,
I will never know fully
if that single light that touches me
might have allowed me moments longer
or if we were destined to meet
always then.

Stuff of Life

Our cells can't tell the difference
between dying and being born.

Death, to genes, seems celebratory
fireworks of first growth
and they alight to dance in the darkness
like they expect a new dawn.

Maybe it is true, maybe
our molecules know more about these
bookends of life than our tiny brains, and
these protein precursors are more
ritual than rational,
reaching beyond that thin wall to whatever
interphase our other existence is.

Or maybe it is a machine
breaking down
and we read into quirks of clumsy biology
to hold off, for a moment more, the thought of simply
not being.

I want, beyond
everything, for it to be
the first one.

2nd Law of Thermodynamics

All things tend toward entropy
because it is easier to simply lie down

let your fingers limp
drop all you held to the floor

ignore the cracking of hardwood and ceramic
surrender to bed

to nature
to knowing this

is how the universe
wants you

Cats in Boxes

He was dead before the box
and every time I opened it to check
I found him the same.

I wish this box was Schrodinger's,
that he might be alive if only I couldn't observe him,
if only life and death weren't the ultimate binary,
if only superposition worked by fucking will.

I might open this box and his muscles
wouldn't be boards, his tongue would pull back
into his mouth and only peek out
through the gap of his missing teeth
when he curled to your side.

He would stretch his old legs in the sun
like he did whenever he awoke, and be
both alive and with me
at the same time.

Supernova 2022

Not a diagnosis, really. Someone
saw the way the stars wobbled, the way they
struggled to march the same rhythm of their youth,
the way they bowed into each other more every year.

For me, this death is coming.
All the rest of my life their light will grow
brighter as ashes of burnt-out suns scatter
across the sky and I will know a time
when the sky had not been an urn.

But I won't. They have always been
dead. They died before
my mother's mother's mother had been a hope.

They died before Rome was two and fell,
before Copernicus knew where the sun truly was,
before anyone looked to our daylight and saw inevitable ash.

Someone will see our star go.
Someone will watch this light become
something more and then something
less, and I will always have been dead.

But maybe, in a thousand years,
someone will let the light of our small star to their eye
and we will share the same rays I did the day I was born
and there, for that moment, I will be born again.

James Wright in Chemistry Class

I bookmarked *Three Steps to the Graveyard*
with indium details. How it's larger than tin
touching *Anacreon's Grave*. How it gives and takes
the energy of other elements – how all elements do.

Students study atoms from flash cards that hold
each page. I use them to bond words of the dead
to me. These symbols of matter
build and break down, making smaller complexities.

Wright toiled over illness and Trakl,
writing letters to Sexton in defiance of letting go.
I closed cadmium's low affinity
where Wright had *A Dream of Burial* anyway.

My feet will likely remain in half-price dress shoes
begging for a little extra black, stained
by unsure freshman hands counting twenty
drops of hydrochloric, shaking forceps of calcium bits.

I think my burial dreams would be anonymous.
Bullets, back alleys, and a box
where my knuckles remain, phosphorous still
making crystals for my parents
to count and lower, rattling awake
dead pens, into a hole.

I search periodic cards to swap cadmium
for something more fitting of endings.
I know carbon, for all it makes
of my hands, works on paper,
but I choose sulfur.

Radiating Black Bodies

They are ideal in their shape, the way they capture
every light shone on them, the way every light is inevitably shone
on them, the way they inevitably reach the same temperature
of any other body they are pressed against.

Touch them as you would
your skin, tell me if there is a difference
in their heat, if there is any part of them that feels
any different than your own body.

Put them next to the white, watch them take everything
white rejects deep into themselves, make the reflected world
their own and meet it equally
as it is given.

I am told this is not real,
this is not truth, but I see them:
black body,
black boy,
black mother.

3rd Law of Motion

Doesn't count for sparks of life, souls, whatever
you call that thing that probably doesn't exist,
that definitely isn't
in the pineal gland.

I mean, what
is an equal and opposite reaction for tying a rope
to door handle and kneeling
until the stars fade in,
until the stars fade out?

Babies.
You say babies. I say
that isn't equal, it isn't even
opposite when a mother breaks down a door
sees it's her baby
on the hardwood.

And, shit,
there are so many more
babies than bodies this month, so
if you're right and a first breath is, by law,
reaction to a final, then
we best finish breathing fast
before more of our babies do.

Spirit and Opportunity

A.
we never expected you to live
so far from home
when the long night came
you slept and we expected
no stretch in the morning light
but you pushed that curtain
fought the creaking joints
slipping memory
carved a path before us
you gave us truth
before we had feet to follow you
you settled into the soft ground
talking to the last
when the night finally came
the soil took you

B.
but you never died
you never stopped searching
      for a home
        for a place to hold
          new feet
             new voices
                new eyes

5th Dimension

Let me hold time like a glass, fill it
to just below the chip in the rim
and never think about it
being a complete life,
every chilled molecule a choice
still vibrating, still asking
glass if it was right. I could change
history by swirling, cause
becomes effect, a choice
can be remade, or
I could put the glass to my lip,
avoid the cutting edge,
steal moments in sips.
I could drink all
but that most stubborn drop
that hangs to the wall and
refuses to leave, then
fill everything and start again.

Ode to Offense

Did you know we are not elastic
    that our words are as solid in collision as lonely rocks
    that make moons about us
    that Tangos are smaller versions of screaming mobs
    that every time a thought escapes warm
        it touches another solid form of some sort
        and something of both will always remain with the other

Offense is something that comes
    from maybe too many collisions
    from maybe too plastic a mind
        maybe to glass a mind
        maybe too often touched a raw edge of a person

and as sick as it may sound there is a perverse beauty
    in the idea of offense
    the idea that we are not floating alone in some void
        that there are tiny rocks
        that there are pieces of other whole worlds that still touch us
        that not everything burns up before
        that somewhere deep inside us we still and always need
            to be with someone else
        that we know the difference between love that takes a piece of us
            and something else that takes a piece of us
            and that we are willing to hold on to what pieces of us we have
    that we know the skin of our worlds
    that the tiniest parts on our skin can become a moon
        to anyone else
    that in some way
        maybe not the greatest way
            we can be part of any world

3rd Law of Thermodynamics

Something about the pinnacle of zero,
absolutism of nothing, the perfection of an ideal
crystal whose atoms are so aligned, so
relaxed, they can finally sleep and hold each other
gently. Really,
it's a lot of science shit.

I guess I should be trying to write this in some sort of form.
How about a sonnet? Such esteem
I have heard them called perfect. Or what about I make this
prose poem in solid blocks, or a visual piece
where all the As line up at the right angles
all the Cs cry for carbon connection and obvious diamond analogy?

I should probably be writing this in metaphors, drawing
comparison to death or anxiety or so much staring at screens
instead of eyes. But I think the most honest use is to say
I don't understand nothingness, like I can't comprehend death,
fully, like I usually can't quite explain life either.

So I'll make this a law about writing;
how I read the crystalline perfection of the masters,
how they make it look effortless,
how I find in the structure of their words a way of measuring my own.

I know that my words, no matter how idealized,
will never reach this most impossible of levels, but,
like the universe,
this is where I will naturally try to go forever.

THANK YOU

If this section giving thanks were to name every person it should, there would be more Thanks than poetry. So if you are not mentioned by name, know that I am still immensely grateful for your support, assistance, and love, I just don't have the space to fit you all.

First, I must thank the wonderful people at Assure Press for giving this book life. They have treated my work with care and respect and continued supporting me and all of their other wonderful writers during what has to be one of the hardest times for small presses. I will be eternally grateful.

I must also thank my Drew Crew, the Get Fresh Crew, you all know who you are, and I love you all. But I will single a few out for their work with me on this piece, specifically. Roberto Carlos Garcia, I thank you for all the advice you gave me and all the time you take to build and maintain such wonderful writing communities. Yesenia Montilla and Lynne McEniry, thank you for your friendship, your inspiration, and your time in reviewing this book. I could not have asked for any better poets or any better people to grace me with their words.

Mike and Adrienne Bross also need some shoutouts on this one for all the time keeping me stable in my insanity and being such great people to bounce ideas off of. Any ideas, really. Your friendship and support have been invaluable. No thanks, whatsoever, goes to Michelle Greco.

And finally, I need to thank my family. Honestly, listing all of you would double this book in size, so just know that I love (most) of you all. If more of my work is lucky enough to find publishing, maybe more of you will be thanked, but I need to thank someone who has been integral in the spirit of this book, more than he could ever know: my father, Max Euston. He fostered in me a love of science, a love of reason, and a love of inquiry. And he showed me how to merge that usually logical, cold world with compassion.

ABOUT THE AUTHOR

Fletch Fletcher is a science teacher, a poet, a brother, a friend, and an observer of how all people connect to everything around them. We need to strive for connection if we are to ever be better than we are.

instagram.com/fletch.fletcher.poet

www.ingramcontent.com/pod-product-compliance
Lightning Source LLC
Chambersburg PA
CBHW021452070526
44577CB00002B/380